1

Dedicated to my friend Goodson and his wife Jackie with the deepest love and affection .....

4

FOREWORD :

You may well say not another monologue on the Book of Job? I encourage you all to stay engaged with this book to the end? What I want to focus on is the response of the LORD God to Job and what he has said and done throughout the Book of Job?

i find the Book of Job fascinating; it has much to say to us all in our time, era and generations? From the onset understand I do not believe the Book of Job is all about the righteous suffering and the reasons as to why they suffer? I believe there are wider themes and concerns than just the suffering of the righteous on show in the Book of Job?

The chapters 38 to 42 illustrate that very clearly to me and I hope they will be etched in your memory as having done the same thing by the end of this monologue? I hope you are ready to both engage with the text of chapters 38 to 42 and also to engage your thinking creatively in seeking to understand these chapters of the Book of Job?

One of the main reasons I have a fondness for the Book of Job is because it origins are non - Israelite and yet it contains much wisdom about the LORD God? Even though it is from a non - Israelite source it is still included in the Canon of the Old Testament; which means a lot lot in terms of the value placed upon it?

Please enjoy the journey I hope we all will undertake as we consider these chapters of the Book of Job?

9

Job 38 to 42.

(CEB)

The LORD answers from a whirlwind.

(38)
(1) " Then the LORD answered Job from the whirlwind:

(2) Who is this darkening counsel with words lacking knowledge?

(3) Prepare yourself like a man;
    I will interrogate you,
        and you will respond to me.

The establishing of order.

(4) Where were you
    when I laid earth's
foundations?
        Tell me if you know.

(5) Who set its measurements?
        Surely you know.
        Who stretched a measuring
tape on it?

(6) On what were its footings
sunk;
        who laid its cornerstone,

(7) while the morning stars
sang in unison

and all the divine beings shouted?

(8) Who enclosed the Sea behind doors
  when it burst forth from the womb,

(9) when I made the clouds its garment,
    the dense clouds its wrap,

(10) when I imposed my limit for it,
    put on a bar and doors

(11) and said, "You may come this far,
    no farther;

here your proud waves stop?"

(12) In your lifetime have you
      commanded the morning
      informed the dawn of its
place

(13) so it would take hold of
earth by its edges
      and shake the wicked out
of it?

(14) Do you turn it over like
clay for a seal,
      so it stands out
      like a colorful garment?

(15) Light is withheld from the wicked,
      the uplifted arm broken.

    The vast beyond.

(16) Have you gone to the sea's sources,
      walked in the chamber of the deep?

(17) Have death's gates been revealed to you;
      can you see the gates of deep darkness?

(18) Have you surveyed earth's expanses?

Tell me if you know
everything about it.

(19) Where's the road to the
place
      where light dwells;
      darkness, where's it
located?

(20) Can you take it to its
territory;
      do you know the paths to
its house?

(21) You know, for you were
born then;
      you have lived such a long
time!

(22) Have you gone to snow's storehouses,
      seen the storehouses of hail

(23) that I have reserved for a time of distress,
      for a day of battle and war?

(24) What is the way to the place
      where light is divided up;
      the east wind scattered over the earth?

Meteorological facts
(25) Who cut a channel for the

downpours
and a way for blasts of thunder
(26) to bring water to uninhabited land,
a desert with no human

(27) to saturate dry wasteland
and make grass sprout?

(28) Has rain a father
who brought forth drops of dew?

(29) From whose belly does ice come;
who gave birth to heaven's frost?

(30) Water hardens like stone;
        the surface of the deep thickens.

(31) Can you bind Pleiades' chains
        or loosen the reins of Orion?

(32) Can you guide the stars
        at their proper times,
           lead the Bear with her cubs?

(33) Do you know heaven's laws,
        or can you impose its rule on earth?

(34) Can you issue an order to the clouds
     so their abundant waters
cover you?

(35) Can you send lightning so that it goes
     and then says to you, " I'm
here."?

(36) Who put wisdom in remote places,
                 or who
gave understanding
     to a rooster?

(37) Who is wise enough to count the clouds,

and who can tilt heaven's
   water containers

(38) so that the dust becomes
mud
       and clods of dirt adhere?

   Lion and raven.

(39) Can you hunt prey for the
lion
       or fill the cravings of lion
cubs?

(40) They lie in their den,
       lie in ambush in their lair.

(41) Who provides food for the
raven

when its young cry to God,
    move about without food?

(39) Mountain goat and doe.

    (1) Do you know when
mountain goats
        give birth;
        do you observe the
birthing of does?

    (2) Can you count the months
of pregnancy;
        do you know when they
give birth?

    (3) They crouch, split open for
their young,

send forth their offspring.

(4) Their young are healthy;
     they grow up in the open country,
       leave and never return.

  Wild donkey.

(5) Who freed the wild donkey,
     loosed the ropes of the onager

(6) to whom I gave the desert as home,
     his dwelling place in the salt flats?

(7) He laughs at clamor of the

town,
     doesn't hear the driver's
shout,

    (8) searches the hills for food
      and seeks any green sprout.

Wild ox.

    (9) Will the wild ox agree to be
your slave,
     or will it spend the night in
your crib?

    (10) Can you bind it with a
rope
      to a plowed row
       will it plow the valley
behind you?

(11) Will you trust it
        because its strength is
great
        so that you can leave your
work to it?

(12) Can you rely on it to bring
back your grain
        to gather into your
threshing floor?

    Ostrich

(13) The ostrich's wings flapping
joyously,
        but her wings and plumage
        are like a stork.

(14) She leaves her eggs on the earth,
        lets them warm in the dust,

    (15) then forgets that
            a foot may crush them
            or a wild animal trample them.

    (16) She treats her young harshly
            as if they were not hers,
            without worrying that her labor
                might be in vain;

(17) God didn't endow her with
sense,
        didn't give her some good
sense.

(18) When she flaps her wings
high,
        she laughs at horse and
rider.

    Horse.

(19) Did you give strength to
the horse,
        clothe his neck with a
mane,

(20) cause him to leap like a
    locust,

his majestic snorting, a
fright?

(21) He paws in the valley,
prances proudly,
          charges at battle
weapons,

(22) laughs at fear, unafraid.
      He doesn't turn away from
the sword;

(23) a quiver of arrows flies by
him,
      flashing spear and dagger.

(24) Excitedly, trembling,

he swallows the ground;
      can't stand still at a
trumpet's blast.

    (25) At a trumpet's sound, he
says, " Aha!"
      smells the battle from
afar,
      hears the officers'
shouting
      and the battle cry.

   Hawk and eagle.

    (26) Is it due to your
understanding
      that the hawk flys,

spreading its wings to the south?

(27) Or at your command does the eagle soar,
      the vulture build a nest on high?

(28) They dwell on an outcropping of rock,
      their fortress on rock's edge.

(29) From there they search for food;
      their eyes notice it from afar,

(30) and their young lap up blood;
    where carcasses lie, there they are. "

(40) The LORD speaks and Job answers.

(1) " The LORD continued
            to respond to Job :

(2) Will the one who disputes with the
            Almighty correct him?
            God's instructor must
answer him.

(3) Job responded to the LORD:

(4) Look, I'm of little worth.

What can I answer you?
   I'll put my hand over my
mouth.

   (5) I have spoken once, I
won't answer;
      twice, I won't do it again.

   A Challenge from the LORD.

   (6) The LORD answered Job
      from the whirlwind:

   (7) Prepare yourself like a
man;
      I will interrogate you,
      and you will respond to me.

(8) Would you question my
justice,
      deem me guilty
      so you can be innocent?

(9) Or do you have an arm
like God;
      can you thunder with a
voice like him?

(10) Adorn yourself
      with splendor and
majesty;
      clothe yourself with
honor and esteem.

(11) Unleash your raging anger;

      look on all the proud and humble them.

(12) Look on all the proud and debase them;

      trample the wicked in their place.

(13) Hide them together in the dust;

      bind their faces in a hidden place.

(14) Then I, even I, will praise you,

for your strong hand has delivered you.

Behemoth.

(15) Look at Behemoth
whom I made along with you;
he eats grass like cattle.

(16) Look, his strength is in thighs,
his power in stomach muscles.

(17) He stiffens his tail like a cedar;

the tendons in his thighs
are tightly woven.

(18) His bones are like bronze
tubes,
　　　　his limbs like iron bars.

(19) He is the first of God's
acts;
　　　　only his maker can come
near him
　　　　with a sword.

(20) Indeed, the hills bring
him tribute,
　　　　places where all the wild
animals play.

(21) He lies under the lotuses,
        under the cover of reed
and marsh.

(22) The lotuses screen him
with shade;
        poplars of the stream
surround him.

(23) If the river surges, he
doesn't hurry;
        he is confident even
though the Jordan
        gushes into his mouth.

(24) Can he be seized by his
eyes?

Can anyone pierce his nose
by hooks? "

(41) Leviathan.

(1) " Can you draw out
Leviathan
        with a hook,
        restrain his tongue with
a rope?

(2) Can you put a cord
through his nose,
        pierce his jaw with a
barb?

(3) Will he beg you at length
        or speak gentle words to
you?

(4) Will he make a pact with you

so that you will take him as a permanent slave?

(5) Can you play with him like a bird

put a leash on him for your girls?

(6) Will merchants sell him;

will they divide him among traders?

(7) Can you fill his hide with darts,

his head with a fishing spear?

(8) Should you lay your hand on him,

      you would never remember the battle.

(9) Such hopes would be delusional;

      surely the sight of him
      makes one stumble.

(10) Nobody is fierce enough to rouse him;

      who then can stand before me?

(11) Who opposes me that I must repay?

Everything under heaven is
mine.

(12) I'm not awed by his limbs,
      his strength, and
impressive form.

(13) Who can remove his outer
garment;
      who can come with a
bridle for him?

(14) Who can open the doors
of his mouth,
      surrounded by frightening
teeth?

(15) His matching scales are

his pride,
    closely locked and sealed.

    (16) One touches another;
        even air can't come
between them.

    (17) Each clings to its pair;
        joined, they can't be
separated.

    (18) His sneezes emit flashes
of light;
        his eyes are like dawn's
rays.

    (19) Shafts of fire shoot

from his mouth;
   like fiery sparks they fly out.

   (20) Smoke pours from his
nostrils
      like a boiling pot over
reeds.

   (21) His breath lights coals;
      a flame shoots from his
mouth.

   (22) Power resides in his neck;
         violence dances before
him.

   (23) The folds of his flesh
stick together;

on him they are tough and
unyielding.

(24) His heart is solid like a
rock,
       hard like a millstone.

(25) The divine beings dread
his rising;
       they withdraw before
his thrashing.

(26) The sword that touches
him
       won't prevail;
       neither will the dart,
spear, nor javelin.

(27) He treats iron as straw,
       bronze as rotten wood.

   (28) Arrows can't make him
flee;
       slingshots he turns to
straw.

   (29) He treats a club like
straw;
       he laughs at the lance's
rattle.

   (30) His abdomen is
       like jagged pottery
shards;

its sharp edges leave a
trail in the mud.

(31) He causes the depths
        to churn like a boiling
pot,
        stirs up the sea
        like a pot of scented oils,

(32) leaves a bright wake
behind him;
        the frothy deep seems
white - haired.

(33) None on earth can
compare to him;
        he is made to be without
fear.

(34) He looks on all the proud;
   he is king over all proud
beasts. "

(42) Job's second response.

(1) " Job answered the LORD:

(2) I know you can do anything;
    no plan of yours
    can be opposed successfully.

(3) You said, " who is this darkening counsel without knowledge?"
    I have indeed spoken about
    things I didn't understand,
    wonders beyond my comprehension.

(4) You said, "Listen and I will
speak;
     I will question you
     and you will inform me."

(5) My ears had heard about
you,
     but now my eyes have seen
you.

(6) Therefore, I relent and
find comfort
     on dust and ashes.

Epilogue

(7) After the LORD had
spoken these words to Job, he

said to Eliphaz from Teman, " I'm angry at you and your two friends because you haven't spoken about me correctly as did my servant Job.

(8) So now, take seven bulls and seven rams, go to my servant Job, and prepare an entirely burned offering for yourselves. Job my servant will pray for you, and I will act favorably by not making fools of you because you didn't speak correctly, as did my servant Job.

(9) Eliphaz from Teman, Bildad from Shu'ah, and Zophar from Na'amah did what the LORD told

them; and the LORD acted favorably toward Job.

(10) Then the LORD changed Job's fortune when he prayed for his friends, and the LORD doubled all Job's earlier possessions.

(11) All his brothers, sisters, and acquaintances came to him and ate food with him in his house. They comforted and consoled him concerning all the disaster the LORD had brought on him, and each one gave him a qesitah and a gold ring.

(12) Then the LORD blessed Job's latter days more than his former ones. He had fourteen thousand sheep, six thousand camels, one thousand yoke of oxen, and one thousand female donkeys.

(13) He also had seven sons and three daughters.

(14) He named one Jemimah, a second Keziah, and the third Keren - happuch.

(15) No women in all the land were as beautiful as Job's daughters, and their father gave an inheritance to them along with

their brothers.

(16) After this, Job lived 140 years and saw four generations of his children.

(17) Then Job died, old and satisfied."

Chapter 38 : The LORD speaks to Job?

The LORD answers from a whirlwind:

(1) " Then the LORD answered Job from
the whirlwind:
  (2) Who is this darkening counsel
      with words lacking knowledge?
  (3) Prepare yourself like a man;
      I will interrogate you,
      and you will respond to me."

At long last in the scope of the entire Book of Job; the LORD God answers Job. A theophany of the whirlwind; or a mighty storm and the LORD God speaking to Job out of it? Up until this point there has been no communication between the LORD God and Job the man from Uz?

In verse three the LORD asks Job to 'prepare yourself like a man', so we have the LORD as creator talking to one of his creatures. In some ways it establishes the ground rules from the beginning of chapter 38; for what follows in chapters 38 to 42? It is the LORD who will interrogate Job and Job will respond to the LORD? All of which is interesting because up until this point in the Book of Job, Job has been trying to get the LORD God to respond to him? So now the LORD has responded to Job but may be not in the way or ways Job ever imagined?

At times we like Job can want to put the LORD in the witness box and get all our questions about the why and wherefore of our lives answered to us by Him? The interesting thing is that from the outset we need to understand that this is not going to happen in chapters 38 to 42? It is rather the LORD God who will be asking the questions and searching questions of Job; that He will expect Job to respond to and answer for himself?

Verse two sums up the view of the LORD God to what Job has been saying and doing thus far in the Book of Job : " Who is this darkening counsel with words lacking knowledge." This in some ways could well be the theme verse which helps us unravel the contents and themes present in chapters 38 to 42 of Job? Essentially the LORD God is saying that Job has muddied the waters of His counsel with his many words without any knowledge? Job has said a lot about his situation and his world and environment in general without there being any real knowledge present in his words? What follows from here on is the LORD God giving Job the knowledge and wisdom and information to inform Job about Himself and His counsel and His ways? In some ways it is a rather damming epitaph of what Job has said, believed and the actions he has done in the Book of Job up until this point in the Book; ' words lacking knowledge'? Job's words have been many but where has been the knowledge that should and could under-gird them and inform them?

In some ways verse one to three set the stage for what will prove to be an interesting encounter between the LORD God and Job in chapters 38 to 42? The LORD God has responded to Job and yet even Job does not know what is coming in his encounter with the LORD God? It is the LORD God who will put Job in the witness box and expect him to respond to His interrogation of him? Job 'will' respond to the interrogation of the LORD God; Job 'will' respond; he will be expected by the LORD God to respond to Him and His questions?

Imagine if you can the LORD God saying that to you or myself and how we would feel and how we would respond to these words if they were spoken to us by the LORD God? So often we are chasing answers from the LORD God to a myriad of questions we have but what would happen if the LORD God put us on the spot and asked us questions instead and searching questions at that? That is the situation that Job is now facing himself at the beginning of chapter 38? He has wanted answers from the LORD God but now he finds the LORD God has some questions that He expects Job to respond to?

The establishing of order: verses 4 to 15..

The LORD God begins His questioning of Job with a series of questions about who keeps the creation in order and running? The LORD God really puts Job on the spot; Job has been expecting to have all his real questions about his life and situation answered but instead he is the one being asked the questions and probing questions at that? From the outset; even in verse four from the question about the earth's foundations one begins to understand that the questions that the LORD God asks of Job; he cannot have any answer or even a glimmer of hope answering for himself?

The reality is that in verses 4 to 15 the questions have to do with creation and the one who keeps the creation in order; the Creator God is on show? It is the big picture of the ordering of the creation of the earth and its various parts that it consists of that is on show in these verses? In some ways there is an echo of Genesis one and two and the creation accounts? Except it does not begin with 'let there be light' but rather the section in verse 15 ends with the question about light and its origins?

The vast beyond : verses 16 to 24.

In some ways these verses 16 to 24 continue the questioning of light and its origins and develop the concepts and ideas related to it? We have the opposite of light; darkness on show as well. Verse 17 is interesting : " Have death's gates been revealed to you; can you see the gates of deep darkness ? " The LORD God is seen now not only as the Creator God but also as the one who controls not only just the creation itself but also life and death within it? Death itself is something which is under His power, authority and control?

The concept of deep darkness contrasts with the concept of light and its origins? The deep darkness and its gates would appear to be related to the gates of death; the gates of deep darkness?

Verse 21 is profound and really appears to make a statement regarding Jo's lack of knowledge, understanding and even wisdom? "You know, for you were born then; you have lived such a long time!" The use of irony in the speech of the LORD God is interesting: He knows that Job is not old enough to have been there at creation and when darkness and light were given their boundaries and the sea and the land were formed? It reveals a Creator God; the LORD God who is timeless and outside and beyond time and space! Job on the other hand is man a human created man and subject to death and also subject to time and space?

Again in these verses we have the concepts of order, creation and the Creator God who is in control on show again? Contrasts between light and darkness abound in verses 16 to 24, death and darkness and light and its origins, creation and its boundaries?

Meteorological Facts : verses 25 to 38.

The Creator God, the LORD God now has some real questions about who controls the rain, lightening and thunder upon the earth for Job? The earth and its creation and the life within it are sustained and even blessed by these very things but who controls them? Again there is a relationship between these verses and the ones previously, in the concept of there being One who brings order and control into the creation? It is not a creation that is driven by chaos and chance and disaster and darkness rather there is order and control in and through its operations and workings?

Verses 31 to 32 involve order not

only in the creation of the earth and its various parts but the stars in the universe are involved as well? " (31) Can you bind Pleiades' chains or loosen the reins of Orion? (32) Can you guide the stars at their proper times, lead the Bear with her cubs? " It is now not only the Creator God; the LORD God and His creation of the earth, its elements and death and life but also now the myriad of stars in the universe? He knows the courses of the stars and directs them as to where they should go in the universe?

These verses are not just about the weather and the control of the Creator God; the LORD God over it but also about the One who sustains , authors and provides the elements necessary to sustain and promote life upon the earth.

Lion and raven: verses 39 to 41.

Now we go from questions by the LORD God about the big picture of the creation, order and the one who is behind it all to questions about who provides and sustains the lion, its young and the raven? There is a real shift that is apparent in the text in these very verses? Again these verses are all caught up with the idea of who sustains, authors and brings control into the creation and its now created animals and creatures.

The LORD God in these verses at the end of chapter 38 is seen as the LORD God who provides even for these two animals the lion and the raven and the young cubs of the lion? The text has shifted from the macro to now the more micro of the creation and deals now with individual parts of the creation? We still have not heard any response from Job to the questions the LORD God has been posing and asking Job if he knows the answers to them?

Chapter 39 : The LORD God continues His questioning of Job.

Mountain goat and doe : verses 1 to 4 .

Again in these four verses we have specific questions for Job; to do with particular creatures of the creation? The mountain goat and their young does this time. Job is asked a question of whether or not he knows when they give birth, the time and the seasons of their pregnancy?

These verse contain a poetic description of the mountain goat and its does; its young and offspring? All of which goes to show that the LORD God knows the times and seasons of even the creatures of His creation?

Wild donkey : verses 5 to 8.

In chapter 39 we again have a

section of verses dealing with a specific creature in the LORD God's creation. This time it is a wild donkey and we find that it is the LORD God who put it in its arid environment in the salt flats? The LORD Gods knowledge goes as far as knowing where to place the creatures of His creation? He knows the character and personality of the wild donkey, how he eats and behaves around people because he remains a wild donkey. He also knows the food the wild donkey needs and survives upon and He makes provision for that as well? Again we are shown a LORD God who is intimately caught up in the lives of the creatures of His creation?

Ostrich : verses 13 to 18.

In some ways this episode with the ostrich and its young shows and reveals that the LORD God has and had a sense of humor when He created creatures? The ostrich forgets and leaves its young in the hot earth, all alone where they could be attacked and eaten and yet they survive this treatment?

Verse 17 is interesting; " God didn't endow her with sense, didn't give her some good sense." In some ways it can be seen that the ostrich has a lack of regard for its young because that is the way the LORD God made the ostrich to be? We again see the LORD God as the Creator God who is intimately involved with the creatures of His creation. He knows them through and through, how they act and their personalities and the particular behaviors that go to make them the creatures of His creation they were meant to be?

Horse : verses 19 to 25.

The questioning of Job by the LORD God continues on unabated in these verses about the whys and wherefores of the horse? Again we see that the LORD God is the One behind the creation of His creature the horse? He knows the character, personality, strengths and weaknesses of the horse; because He created the horse itself?

Also the fact that the horse can be used in the battles of war is worth noting? Its the LORD God who again created the horse to be a creature who can carry men into the battles of warfare? We see graphically that the LORD God has endowed the horse with the ability to both endure and even enjoy going into the battles that are involved in warfare?

Hawk and eagle : verses 26 to 30.

At the end of chapter 39 again we are given an insight into the character, makeup and how an animal that is a created creature functions? This time it is the 'birds of the air'; the hawk and the eagle, two of the highest forms of bird life that have been created by the LORD God? The LORD God has created them and also endowed them with particular characteristics which make them unique as ' birds of the air'. For example the LORD God is the One who has given them the ability to see their prey from high up in the atmosphere when they are in flight? The questions continue and are based on particular parts of the creation of the LORD God; particular creatures He has created and their unique characteristics He has endowed them with?

Chapter 40 : The LORD speaks and Job answers : verses 1 to 5.

" (1) The LORD continued to respond to Job:

(2) Will the one who disputes with the Almighty correct him?
        God's instructor must answer him."

        The LORD God continues to respond to Job and may well be we need to understand that throughout the Book of Job; Job had wanted the LORD God to respond to him and his situation? Its interesting that the word ' disputes with the Almighty correct him ? ' is used? In the end the LORD God is dealing with or attempting to deal with the dispute or case Job had been seeking to bring to His attention.

        ' God's instructor must answer him '; is an interesting turn of phrase and shows Job as the one seeking to instruct God?

The LORD God now Job who has acted as though he is the instructor of the LORD God will answer questions posed to him by the LORD God?

" (3) Job responded to the LORD :
(4) Look, I'm of little worth.
      What can I answer you?
      I "ll put my hand over my mouth.
(5) I have spoken once, I won't answer;
      twice, I won't do it again."

Job says he is responding to the LORD God and yet his response to the LORD God is that he in the end will not respond to Him? Job seems to realize the folly of responding to the questions that the LORD God has peppered him with. Job recognizes that he does not have any valid answers to the questions of the LORD God? Because he realizes he does not have any real answers to the questions of the LORD God and the major questions He has already posed for Job to answer? Job has decided it is better for him to be quiet in the face of these incessant questions from the LORD God?

A challenge from the LORD : verses 6 to 14?

We have the theophany again; of the LORD God speaking to Job out of a storm or whirlwind (verse 6)?   As well again the LORD God is preparing to interrogate Job the man; he will again be asking Job question upon question. The LORD God ignores Job's statement that he does not what to say to Him (verses 4 and 5) ? In verse 7 b we have the following statement from the LORD God ' ... and you will respond to me'. The LORD God is again going to interrogating Job and He has the expectation that Job ' will ' respond to His interrogation of him and the question after question from Him?

Verses 8 to 14 appear to get to the heart of the LORD God's reason for questioning Job and wanting him to respond to Himself?
" (8) Would you question my justice,
        deem me guilty

so you can be innocent?
(9) Or do you have an arm like God;
        can you thunder with a voice like
him?
    (10) Adorn yourself
        with splendor and majesty;
        clothe yourself with honor and
esteem.
    (11) Unleash your raging anger;
        look on all the proud and humble
them;
    (12) Look on all the proud and debase
them,
        trample the wicked in their place.
    (13) Hide them together in the dust;
        bind their faces in a hidden place.
    (14) Then I, even I, will praise you,
        for your strong hand has delivered
you."

    Verse 8 sets up the whole reason for
the LORD God's responding to Job; He
believes Job is in the end questioning His
justice and the way He deals with His
created beings ? This may or may not be

caught up with the whole idea of suffering and may well be the idea of why the good suffer injustice seemingly at the hands of the LORD God?

There is yet; more to the statements in these particular verses it is not just a questioning of the justice of the LORD God regards suffering and even the suffering of the righteous? In the end it is a case of Job seemingly wanting to place himself in the position of the LORD God Himself? It deals with the heart of the matter before re Genesis account of the Fall; where the created human being wants to be like the LORD God in power, authority and knowledge? It gets at the tendency of man to want to play the role of the LORD God?

Verse 14 states that if Job truly could fill the position of the LORD God then the LORD God Himself would indeed praise him? The reason would be ' for your strong hand has delivered you'; rather than the LORD God being the savior and deliverer of Job he would fulfill both of these functions by himself? Thereby he would have made his case to be the LORD God and take the position and place of the LORD God?

Behemoth : verses 15 to 24 .

The Lord God in His disputation with Job presents the argument of how He both controls, leads, authors and created one of the most fearsome beasts or creatures of the time period or era? This fearsome creature was one of the first creatures created by the LORD God: ' (16) He is the first of God's acts; only his maker can come near him with a sword.' The Behemoth is both feared and revered by the other animals and creatures and even by the creation itself?

Verses 15 to 24 described the power, authority and creative force of the Behemoth in poetic form? He is one of

of the creatures created by the LORD god
who should be feared by other creatures and
yet is both known by and under the control of
the LORD God? Humans cannot control
Behemoth but the LORD God created him
and also has control of him ?

Chapter 41 : Leviathan : verses 1 to 34.

Herr again in this chapter we are given both questions to job and a poetic description of one of the periods most feared creatures? May have been in reality a crocodile; yet that is at most a guess and not a given? The name Leviathan in the Word of God is caught up with a mighty beast or creature of chaos? This creature or beast of chaos is in contrast to the order, control and creative force and power of the LORD God that has been on show thus far? It may well be that Leviathan rather than being an actual creature or beast represents the forces of chaos and the chaotic forces that can be let loose within the creation unless the LORD God was involved with the creation intimately?

Whatever is the way you see Leviathan , the fact and reality as powerful, fearsome and full of chaos as he is, he is still under the power and authority of the LORD God? Even Leviathan as powerful and as full of fearsome power as he is presented in these verses is subject to the LORD God? There would seem to be a contrast between the power and fear and authority of Leviathan and that of the LORD God?

In some ways Behemoth and Leviathan are worst - case scenarios and the most fearsome and powerful creatures the LORD God has created. Yet even both of them are subject to the LORD God and His power and authority over them and the whole of the creation?

Verse 11 'who opposes me that I must repay? Everything under heaven is mine.', is a clear statement and a question at the same time from the LORD God. Even Leviathan cannot oppose the LORD God, then the question is can Job successfully oppose the LORD God if the fearsome Behemoth and Leviathan cannot oppose Him? The second part of the verse is interesting ' Everything under heaven is mine'; everything, created beings and creation under heaven and heavens rightfully belongs to the LORD God? He is the rightful owner of everything under heaven, including Behemoth, Leviathan and human beings like Job and his family?

Chapter 42 : Job's second response : verses 1 - 6.

" (1) Job answered the LORD:
(2) I know you can do anything;
no plans of yours
can be opposed successfully.
(3) You said, " Who is this darkening
counsel without knowledge?"
I have indeed spoken about
things I didn't understand;
wonders beyond my comprehension.
(4) You said, " Listen and I will speak;
I will question you
and you will inform me."
(5) My ears had heard about you,
but now my eyes have seen you.
(6) Therefore, I relent and find comfort
on dust and ashes."

Job had said previously in chapter 40 that he would not respond again to the LORD God when He required him to respond to Him? Yet in these verses Job responds to what the LORD

God has been saying, stating, presenting and making known to him?

Verse three is particularly telling in that Job recognizes now that he has had things explained to him that were not in his comprehension before? The LORD God has asked home a number of probing rhetorical questions, questions that Job could never answer for himself and thereby given him knowledge about the LORD God he didn't possess before this encounter with the LORD God? This is summed up in verse 5 " My ears had heard about you, but now my eyes have seen you." In the past relationship with the LORD God Job was going on the information that had been shared and revealed to him about the LORD God, yet now he has had the encounter with the LORD God he had been seeking, finally in the end all has been revealed? Job now has gained first - hand knowledge of the LORD God he has worshiped and served all his life. The knowledge and wisdom and information that Job has gained about the LORD God has transformed his entire life and world view and even his thought processes about the LORD God?

In the end in verse 6 Job turns away from the position of being an adversary of the LORD God that he had taken up previously in the Book against the LORD God? He now has knowledge which transforms and changes himself and the way and ways he views his life and situation? The dust and ashes had been there as a sign of mourning in chapter 3 of the Book of Job but now it is a sign of repentance and grief over the mistaken way he had previously viewed the LORD God throughout the Book of Job?

Epilogue : verses 7 to 16.

In verses 7 to 9 we find the LORD God asking Job to act as a mediator between the LORD God and Job's three friends , Eliphaz, Bildad and

Zophar? From the perspective of the LORD god they are seen as not having represented what has happened to Job correctly throughout the Book of Job? The LORD God asks Job to offer a sacrifice for his three friends and also to pray for the LORD God's forgiveness for their folly and misinformation and distortion of the intent and name of the LORD God throughout the Book of Job.

Also it is worth noting that Job is now in chapter 42, seen by the LORD God as being the servant of the LORD God? The LORD God no longer just sees him as just a man questioning Him and His purposes and authority but He now sees him as His servant? All of which goes to show that Job was and has always been in right standing throughout the Book of Job with the LORD God? It is the three friends of Job who have not been in right standing with the LORD God and have not represented Him correctly to Job at all?

In verse 9 ; ' and the LORD acted favorably toward Job'; the LORD acted favorably to job, heard his prayers for his three friends and accepted the sacrifice that he had offered on their behalf? Verse 10; 'Then the LORD changed Job's fortune when he prayed for his three friends, and the LORD doubled all Job's earlier possessions.' Verses 11 to 16 fill out the detail as to the blessings from the LORD God that Job received from Him.

Verse 11 sums up the reality that it was not just material blessings that Job received from the LORD God but also restored relationships with both his family and the community - at - large. Job was no longer on the outer but now was embraced, celebrated and loved by both his family members and the community - at - large?

Verse 17 ; 'Then Job died, old and satisfied .' is a great conclusion both to the Book of Job and chapters 38 to 42 and our discussion of them.

97

EPILOGUE :

The title of this monologue is ' God's Response to Job ' : Job 38 to 42; as we have seen the response of the LORD God to Job was not what Job expected? In some ways I think the response of the LORD God to Job surprised him and even confounded him? It may well have blind - sided him and to me the response of the LORD God to Job comes out of left - field? The LORD God does not respond in the way Job expects Him to but also He does not respond in the way and ways we as readers of the Book of Job would have been expecting Him to respond to Job as well?

With the LORD God we can want Him to respond to ourselves in a particular way and yet when he does respond in His own way and ways we might not be ready to accept His response to us? Also much like Job we want all the answers to our deepest questions about life, faith and the ways of the LORD God and we want them now? The response of the LORD God to us when it comes may also confound, surprise and even amaze us; much like the response of the LORD God did with Job?

In the end the message of chapters 38 to 42 of Job is that the LORD God is indeed the LORD God and He brokers no rivals and He does not have to answer to anybody? He is the LORD God who holds all things in the universe, the earth and the creation together and He sustains them and He provides and manages every part of it?

Lightning Source UK Ltd.
Milton Keynes UK
UKHW020648110619
344160UK00009B/187/P